1.6 Million
African American Quilters:
Survey, Sites, and a Half-Dozen Art Quilt Blocks

by Kyra E. Hicks

Black Threads Press
Arlington, Virginia

ISBN: 978-0-9824796-7-4
Library of Congress Control Number: 2010911236

Library of Congress subject headings:
1. Quilting – United States – History
2. African American quiltmakers
3. African American quilts – Bibliography
4. Patchwork – Patterns

Cover Art: Francine Haskins, *Three Quiltin' Friends,* 2010

Cover Design: ManjariGraphics

Edited by Kristin P. Walinski, Scribe On Demand Editorial Services

Lovingly dedicated to my sister,
Iyisa Kathaleen Hicks
(1970 – 2010)

Congratulations to
Storytellers in Cloth,
an annual African American quilting retreat
organized by Michelle Lewis and Gloria Douglas.
Happy 15th Anniversary!

1.6 Million African American Quilters:
Survey, Sites, and a Half-Dozen Art Quilt Blocks

Contents

Introduction

During the 2000 presidential election between Governor George W. Bush and Vice President Al Gore, I stitched a narrative quilt titled "I Count," showing a Black woman standing in front of an American flag. To me, the quilt symbolized the importance of one person's vote and participating in a national election or activity.

I didn't realize then that counting and documenting would become a cornerstone for activities that I love and that I hope are useful to others. In 2003, my book *Black Threads: An African American Quilting Sourcebook* sought to document two hundred years of Black quilting history.

This booklet is my latest effort. The focus is on counting and documenting today's Black quilters. *1.6 Million African American Quilters* is composed of four sections:

1. **Counting Quilters**. This chapter quantifies the number of Black quilters based on the latest Quilting in America™ industry survey. U.S. Census data is used to estimate Black quilters by state.

2. **Black Quilters in Cyberspace**. This section is the most comprehensive resource to date on websites, blogs, and YouTube videos focused primarily on African American quilters and guilds. Also included in the more than 270 references are selected textile artists, doll makers, fabric designers, and non-U.S. quilters.

3. **Art Quilt Blocks**. In celebration of 1.6 million African American quilters, artist Francine Haskins has designed six block patterns.

4. **Bibliography**. This section includes references to selected books, articles, exhibit catalogs, dissertations, papers, and films about Black quilters. Many of the references are annotated. Particularly exciting are the references to African American quilters and guilds that have self-published books about their quiltmaking.

I hope quilters, art historians, exhibit curators, and potential quilt collectors will enjoy *1.6 Million African American Quilters*.

Kyra E. Hicks
Arlington, VA

Counting Quilters

U.S. Quilting Industry

U.S. quilters spent $3.58 billion on their stitching passion, according to the 2010 Quilting in America™ survey, an ongoing industry study by *Quilters Newsletter* magazine and in cooperation with the International Quilt Market & Festival. The goals of the Quilting in America surveys are to measure quilters' time and monetary investment in this cherished hobby as well as identify and describe key quilter segments. Six surveys (one every three years) have been conducted since 1994.[1]

Table 1. U. S. Quilting Industry by Households (HH)

	Quilters as % of U.S. HH	Avg. Dollars Spent Per HH	# of U.S. Quilters (millions)	Industry Value (billions)
2010	14.0%	$219.00	21.29	$ 3.58
2006	17.0%	$172.29	27.74	$ 3.29
2003	15.0%	$139.70	21.31	$ 2.27
2000	15.1%	$118.02	19.76	$ 1.83
1997	12.2%	$100.64	13.84	$ 1.21
1994	14.7%	$110.29	15.50	$ 1.55

According to the survey, the results of which are shown in Table 1, U.S. quilters represent 14 percent of all households nationally, or slightly more than 21 million quilters in 2010. To put this in perspective, the number of U.S. quilters is about the size of the population of Australia![2] The number of U.S. quilter households declined 23 percent between 2006 and 2010. The prolonged recession and record unemployment were likely major factors in discouraging thousands of quilters from investing in the

---

[1] Quilting in America™ - 2010, 2006, 2003, 2000, 1997, 1994 surveys. To purchase detailed Quilting in America™ survey results, contact Megan Smith, Creative Crafts Group, at msmith@creativecraftsgroup.com. The author wishes to thank Tina Battock, Vice President and Group Publisher, Creative Crafts Group, for her gracious and unfailing assistance over the years in sharing insights about African American quilter statistics.

[2] Wikipedia, "Demographics of Australia," accessed June 14, 2010,, en.wikipedia.org/wiki/Demographics_of_Australia.

hobby at the same levels they had in previous years. Some casual quilters may have shifted to other crafts.

Dedicated Quilters

During the same time period, the number of "dedicated quilters" increased. Dedicated quilters, as defined by Quilting in America™ surveys, are those who spend more than six hundred dollars per year on quilt-related purchases (e.g., fabrics, sewing machines, classes, magazines, and books).

According to the 2010 survey, the average "dedicated quilter" is a sixty-two-year-old woman, the highest average age since the survey began in 1994. She is college educated and enjoys a household income of $91,602. She spends an average of $2,442 a year on her quilting passion. Her fabric stash is large, as she has purchased an average of 93.6 yards of fabric in the last twelve months.

The dedicated quilter has been stitching quilts for an average of sixteen years. Forty-four percent of dedicated quilters prefer traditional quiltmaking, while fifty percent enjoy making both traditional and contemporary-style quilts. Eighty-five percent are privileged to have a room solely for sewing and quilt-making activities.

The dedicated quilter purchased an average of 4.4 quilting books in the last year and, coincidently, subscribed to or read an average of 4.4 quilting magazines to learn new tips and techniques, find creative inspiration, and learn about new quilt-related products.

She likely owns a personal computer and regularly accesses the Internet. Twenty-eight percent are even members of Facebook!

Table 2. U.S. Dedicated Quilters (DQ) 1994 - 2010

	DQ as % U.S. Quilters	# of DQ (millions)	Avg. Spend	% of Industry Spend	Avg. Age	Avg. Years Quilting
2010	6.2%	1.320	$ 2,442	69.0%	62	16.0
2006	4.7%	1.304	$ 2,304	88.0%	59	13.5
2003	5.2%	1.172	$ 1,934	94.7%	58	12.3
2000	6.0%	1.185	$ 1,556	94.0%	55	11.2
1997	4.9%	0.678	$ 1,430	77.0%	54	10.7
1994	5.4%	0.837	$ 1,203	50.0%	52	10.5

Source: Quilting in America surveys.

1.6 Million African American Quilters

According to Tina Battock, Vice President and Group Publisher for the company that sponsors the Quilting in America surveys, African American quilters represented 7.8 percent of U.S. quilter households in 2010, up from 5.1 percent in 2000.[3]

As a result of the Quilting in America surveys, several points about African American quilters can be made:

- Currently, there are 1.6 million African American quilters.
- In the last decade, the number of Black quilters grew 65 percent; the total number of U.S. quilters grew by only 8 percent.
- African American quilting households spend $279.8 million annually on quilting, up nearly 300 percent since 2000.
- Most African American quilters are fifty-five years old or older.
- According to the 2010 survey, 5.9 percent of Black quilters are eighteen to twenty-four years old; 6.5 percent are twenty-five to thirty-four years old; 7.3 percent are thirty-five to forty-four years old; 67.9 percent are fifty-five years old and older; and 2.8 percent declined to give their age.[4]
- According to the 2010 survey results, 4.5 percent of dedicated quilters, or 59,410 quilters, are African American.[5]

Table 3. African American Quilting Households (HH)

	# of Quilting HH which are Black *	# of Black Quilting HH	# of Black Quilters	Total Dollars Spent by Black Quilting HH
2010	7.8%	1,277,640	1,660,932	$ 279,803,160
2006	7.1%	1,358,585	1,969,948	$ 234,070,610
2003	6.1%	984,601	1,289,827	$ 137,548,760
2000	5.1%	793,588	1,007,857	$ 93,659,256
1997	3.6%	433,152	498,125	$ 43,592,417

Source: * Quilting in America surveys. 1994 data is not available.

Assumptions: The number of quilters per household and the average dollars spent per household for Black quilters are the same as for U.S. quilters. More research is needed to verify this assumption.

---

[3] Tina Battock, telephone call with the author, July 8, 2010; email to the author, January 26, 2001.

[4] Tina Battock, telephone interview with the author, July 8, 2010.

[5] Tina Battock, email to the author, June 21, 2010.

Can you imagine? 1.6 million African American quilters! This is equal to the number of Wal-Mart employees worldwide in 2005.[6] It is also about the size of the African American population of Maryland in 2008.[7]

African American quilters are not a homogenous group. We are traditional quilters and art quilters, narrative quilters, and abstract quilters. We are lapsed, beginner, casual, intermediate, and expert quilters. Some of us quilt alone and have no guild affiliation. Some of us are paying members of professional quilting organizations. We are self-taught or regular quilt-workshops attendees. Some of us are quilt teachers. We belong to quilting circles, mixed-race quilting groups, and African American quilting guilds. Some of us learned to quilt from family members, from the Girl Scouts, from Jack & Jill, from a church group, from a PBS television quilting show or a quilt magazine. Some of us learned to quilt while incarcerated. Some of us create quilts to celebrate life events, to make a political statement, to honor God, or to memorialize a loved one who has passed away naturally or from AIDS, breast cancer, or even street violence. We stitch quilts to keep, to give as personal gifts or as part of community service. Some of us are commissioned to make quilts. Some of us sell our quilts in person or on eBay or Etsy.

Just where are 1.6 million African American quilters located? The Black quilter population is assumed to be proportional to African American population figures by state, in the absence of specific quilt industry data.

African American Quilters by State

According to the U.S. Census Statistical Abstract for July 2008, the U.S. population was 304 million. Black Americans numbered thirty-nine million or 12.8 percent of the population.[8] Using these numbers, we can estimate that:

- Black quilters are an estimated 0.5 percent of the U.S. population.
- Black quilters represent 4.3 percent of African Americans in the United States.

---

[6] *Wikipedia*, "Wal-Mart," accessed July 25, 2010, en.wikipedia.org/wiki/Wal-Mart.

[7] See Table 4.

[8] Resident Population by Race, Hispanic Origin, and State: 2008, U.S. Census Bureau, Washington, DC, July 2008. See also www.census.gov/compendia/statab/cats/population.html.

Table 4. Estimating the Number of African American Quilters by State

		Est. Black Population Jul-08 *	State as % Black Pop Jul-08 *	Est. Black Quilters by State	Est. Black Dedicated Quilters
	United States	**39,058,834**		**1,660,932**	**59,410**
1	New York	3,362,736	8.6%	142,996	5,115
2	Florida	2,916,174	7.5%	124,007	4,436
3	Georgia	2,907,944	7.4%	123,657	4,423
4	Texas	2,898,143	7.4%	123,240	4,408
5	California	2,451,453	6.3%	104,245	3,729
6	North Carolina	1,991,654	5.1%	84,693	3,029
7	Illinois	1,919,701	4.9%	81,633	2,920
8	Maryland	1,658,422	4.2%	70,522	2,523
9	Virginia	1,546,444	4.0%	65,761	2,352
10	Michigan	1,424,595	3.6%	60,579	2,167
11	Louisiana	1,410,457	3.6%	59,978	2,145
12	Ohio	1,382,358	3.5%	58,783	2,103
13	Pennsylvania	1,342,571	3.4%	57,091	2,042
14	South Carolina	1,275,815	3.3%	54,253	1,941
15	New Jersey	1,255,868	3.2%	53,404	1,910
16	Alabama	1,229,787	3.1%	52,295	1,871
17	Mississippi	1,092,588	2.8%	46,461	1,662
18	Tennessee	1,042,811	2.7%	44,344	1,586
19	Missouri	679,223	1.7%	28,883	1,033
20	Indiana	578,088	1.5%	24,583	879
21	Massachusetts	455,880	1.2%	19,386	693
22	Arkansas	450,037	1.2%	19,137	685
23	Connecticut	361,879	0.9%	15,388	550
24	Wisconsin	341,723	0.9%	14,531	520
25	Kentucky	329,225	0.8%	14,000	501
26	Wash DC	322,021	0.8%	13,694	490
27	Oklahoma	289,993	0.7%	12,332	441
28	Arizona	270,159	0.7%	11,488	411
29	Washington	245,000	0.6%	10,418	373
30	Minnesota	238,531	0.6%	10,143	363
31	Colorado	211,249	0.5%	8,983	321
32	Nevada	210,677	0.5%	8,959	320
33	Delaware	182,890	0.5%	7,777	278
34	Kansas	172,342	0.4%	7,329	262
35	Iowa	80,516	0.2%	3,424	122
36	Nebraska	80,174	0.2%	3,409	122
37	Oregon	76,109	0.2%	3,236	116
38	Rhode Island	66,847	0.2%	2,843	102
39	West Virginia	64,987	0.2%	2,763	99
40	New Mexico	59,009	0.2%	2,509	90

Table 4. **Estimating the Number of African American Quilters by State** (cont.)

		Est. Black Population Jul-08 *	State as % Black Pop Jul-08 *	Est. Black Quilters by State	Est. Black Dedicated Quilters
41	Hawaii	39,620	0.1%	1,685	60
42	Utah	34,880	0.1%	1,483	53
43	Alaska	29,274	0.1%	1,245	45
44	New Hampshire	16,015	0.04%	681	24
45	Idaho	14,470	0.04%	615	22
46	Maine	13,588	0.03%	578	21
47	South Dakota	9,185	0.02%	391	14
48	North Dakota	6,956	0.02%	296	11
49	Wyoming	6,884	0.02%	293	10
50	Montana	6,504	0.02%	277	10
51	Vermont	5,378	0.01%	229	8
	Totals	**39,058,834**	**100%**	**1,660,932**	**59,410**

Source: * Resident Population by Race, Hispanic Origin, and State: 2008,
U.S. Census Bureau, Washington, DC, July 2008.
See also www.census.gov/compendia/statab/cats/population.html

Black Quilters in Cyberspace

The Women of Color Quilters Network emerged in 1986 from a simple classified ad Carolyn Mazloomi placed in the February issue of the *Quilter's Newsletter Magazine.* She wanted to correspond with other "Black quilters worldwide" and asked quiltmakers to get in touch with her. At its peak, the Network included 1,700 members.[9]

Today, quilters of color are connecting in a variety of ways traditional and contemporary. We're still meeting in local church fellowship halls, at local community centers, in libraries, and in our homes. We are still sharing quilt patterns, participating in round robins, arranging trips to local fabric stores, and smiling as folks ooh-and-ahh at our latest quilt held-up high during Show-and-Tell.

We are also meeting online. We have individual or group websites showcasing our recent creative endeavors. We post guild newsletters and updates. We use the online space to document our work or share insights into our creative inspirations. We post camera-phone images of our kids and significant others too. We network with quilt makers worldwide.

Following is one of the most comprehensive aggregations of African American quilter websites, blogs, videos, and interviews ever published.

This list was gathered between May and August 2010. The main criterion is that the site celebrates the voice of the quilter, whether speaking for himself or herself or being interviewed.

The list is alphabetical. While most references are for quilters, I have included the occasional textile artist, doll maker, or other craftsperson whose work seems inspired by a quilting tradition or whose work can be an input into the quilt-making process, such as a fabric designer. The list includes Black quilters across the Diaspora, not just in the United States.

Some sites offer items for sale. There is no implied endorsement of any site on this list. Some of the sites were updated as recently as yesterday, and other sites were last updated a year or two ago. Each is included so we celebrate the broadest range of Black quilters in cyberspace.

---

[9] Patricia C. Pongracz and Carolyn Mazloomi. <u>Threads of Faith: Recent Works from the Women of Color Quilters Network</u>. (New York: Gallery of the American Bible Society, 2004). p. 13.

Websites, Blogs, Videos and Interviews

Karima Abdusamad
osmanart.net/karima1.html

Aleeda
fiberquest.blogspot.com

Alice Alexander
sewcreative-alma103.blogspot.com

Hattie Bell Anderson (1894–1990)
news.pcc.edu/2007/09/cascade-gets-historic-quilt-donation-from-local/

Winnie Anderson, Winnie's Quilt Video
youtube.com/watch?v=7zuxnYG-rkk

Gwendolyn Aqui
passagewaysstudio.com/aqui/aqui.htm#

Aunt Be Quilts
auntbequilts.com

Lauren Austin
thatblackgirlart.com   blackgirlart.blogspot.com

Malene B., carpet designer
maleneb.com

Cathleen Richardson Bailey
cathleenbailey.com

Patricia Batiste-Brown
artbrokeress.com/pat.html

Alice Beasley
alicebeasley.com

Marquetta Bell-Johnson, author, *Hand-Dyed Quilts*
atikaart.com

Cuesta Benberry (1923–2007)
allianceforamericanquilts.org/treasures/main.php?id=4

Mary Lee Bendolph, The Quilters of Gee's Bend, Alabama Clip 4
youtube.com/watch?v=8BxGvFxSjYE

Sandy Benjamin-Hannibal
ebonyquilters.com/Sandy%20Benjamin-Hannibal.htm

Wycliffe Lincoln Bennett
lincsart.com

Mozell Benson, 2001 NEA National Heritage Fellow
nea.gov/honors/heritage/fellows/fellow.php?id=2001_02

Jerome Bias, furniture maker
jeromebiasfurnituremaker.com

Lillian Blades, mixed-media artist from Nassau, Bahamas
lillianblades.com
youtube.com/watch?v=ftwEw-xjpxk

Pauline Bloomfield, mixed-media artist in East Midlands, England
axisweb.org/seCVPG.aspx?ARTISTID=6598

Edward Bostick
africanamericanquilts-bostick.com

Karen Boutte, author, *Delightful Diva Designs*
karenboutte.com

Tammie Bowser, author, *Simply Amazing Quilted Photography*
mosaicquilt.com

Diana Bracy
dianabracy.com

O.V. Brantley
ovbrantley.com   africancanvasquilts.wordpress.com

Tina Williams Brewer, author, *Guided by the Ancestors*
tinawilliamsbrewer.com

Sheila Bridges, Harlem Toile de Jouy fabric designer
sheilabridges.com

Earthleen Briggs, Ethnic Quilts and Fabric Shop
ethnicquilts-fabrics.com

Willa Brigham, Willa Brigham on Quilting (video)
youtube.com/watch?v=Dr0ISBm01hk

E. Aminata Brown, designer
babablanket.com

Jocelynn Brown, *Detroit News* Crafting Blog
apps.detnews.com/apps/blogs/craftblog

Peche Brown
renaissancepburg.com/Quilts.html

Wendell George Brown
wendellgeorgebrown.net

Willie Mae Brown, Mother Brown Quilt Video
youtube.com/watch?v=fT7Z_BB79wA

Brown Girl Quilts
browngirlquilts.blogspot.com

Adrienne Bryant, Adrienne's Quilt Video
youtube.com/watch?v=HQjp8XQjJ_o

Paul Buford (1918 – 2000)
sabinahistory.org/paulbuford.htm

Bisa Butler
web.mac.com/mailissabutler

Sherry Ann Byrd
quiltstoriesbysherryann.blogspot.com

Cozbi A. Cabrera
cozbi.com

Viola Williams Canady (1922 – 2009)
allianceforamericanquilts.org/qsos   or go directly with: bit.ly/aXXuh0

Carol
jehjirehspiritquilts.blogspot.com

Laura Casmore
lauragirlsplace.blogspot.com

Cynthia H. Catlin
quiltsonthewall.com/quiltArtists/catlinNew.html

Cindy Cephas
quiltsbycc.com

Geneva Chapman, Geneva's Quilt Video
youtube.com/watch?v=THCBRXxFUQU

Rosie Chapman, fabric postcards
web.mac.com/mizrosie

Irene E. Childress
gracefulstitches.net

Aleathia Chisolm
eclecticquilts.com

City Girl Quilts
citygirlquilts.blogspot.com

Chris Clark
chrisclarkart.com

Rachel D. K. Clark
rdkc.com

Marion Coleman
marioncoleman.com   marioncoleman.blogspot.com

Joyce E. Braxton Coley, quilts and poems
seldomidle.blogspot.com

Donnette A. Cooper
allianceforamericanquilts.org/qsos   or go directly with: bit.ly/b56y0S

Crafty Sistah
craftysistah.com

Lauren Cross, The Skin Quilt Project (film)
skinquiltproject.com

Carolyn Crump
justlookin.com/bios/ccrump.htm

Adriene Cruz
adrienecruz.com

Nadine M. Cuffy
fiberinspired.com

Michael A. Cummings
michaelcummings.com

Michele David
creole-creations.com
allianceforamericanquilts.org/qsos   or go directly with: bit.ly/cCrZQt

Nike Davies-Okundaye, Nigeria textile artist
nikeart.com

Karen Davis, blogging about her quiltmaking since 2004
karoda.typepad.com

Francelise Dawkins
francelisedawkins.com

Ina Dews
www.museum.state.il.us/pressroom/index.html?NPR=503

Marita Dingus, mixed-media artist
maritadingus.com

Tonya Dyce
paintedthreads.com

"Edith," from *Mrs. Bobbins*, a quilt-themed comic strip
pickledish.kcstar.com

Rhonda Edwards
allianceforamericanquilts.org/qsos   or go directly with: bit.ly/beIKDH

Ken Ellis
anatomicallycorrect.org/KenEllis.htm

Nora Ezell (1917 – 2007), 1992 NEA National Heritage Fellow
nea.gov/honors/heritage/fellows/fellow.php?id=1992_06

Gyleen X. Fitzgerald, author, *Poetry and Patchwork*
colourfulstitches.com

Cherryl Floyd-Miller
cherrylfloyd-miller.blogspot.com

Kathleen Flowers
youtube.com/watch?v=In2ZY0aRw_s   bit.ly/d7nFn1

L'Merchie Frazier, L'Merchie Frazier and her Inaugural Quilt video
youtube.com/watch?v=AZf-aH4Q9Vs

Jean Freeman
edsloanfamily.org/quilts.htm

"YES, WE DID!"

"Edith" is one character in the funny comic strip Mrs. Bobbins, illustrated by Julia Icenogle. You can see more comics at Pickledish.kcstar.com. Courtesy of the Kansas City Star Quilts.

Marjorie Diggs Freeman
allianceforamericanquilts.org/qsos or go directly with: bit.ly/bwLGNs

Roland Freeman, the Group for Cultural Documentation
tgcd.org

Willa Hill Fuller
willawags.blogspot.com

Laura R. Gadson
gadsongallery.blogspot.com   thegadsongallery.com

Joan M. E. Gaither
joangaither.com

Doreen Gittens, Jamaican-born, British textile designer
archipelagotextiles.co.uk

Valerie S. Goodwin
quiltsbyvalerie.com   quiltsbyvalerie.blogspot.com

Marilyn Y. Gore
stitchingandstirring.com

Katrina Gorman
katrinagormandesigns.com

Zelda Grant, author, *Fabric Crafts: 15 Creative Projects and Home Accents You Can Make*
chilindemud.org

Deborah Grayson
graysonstudios.com   dgbquilts.wordpress.com

Deonna Todd Green, Quilts and Human Rights (video)
youtube.com/watch?v=zbij1g1M154

Myrah Brown Green, author, *Pieced Symbols: Quilt Blocks from the Global Village*
myrahbrowngreen.com

Karen Hampton
kdhampton.com

Sandra M. Hankins
studiosanteena.com

Rosaland Hannibal
soulfulcreating.blogspot.com

Laurel K. Harper
livelystitches.blogspot.com

Carole Harris
charris-design.com

Phyllis J. Harris
phyllisjharris.com

Virginia R. Harris
cottonwoodshadow.com/films/virginia.php

April Harrison, South Carolina painter with a "quilt-like quality"
aprilsongallery.com

Peggie Hartwell
peggiehartwell.com

Sandy Barrett Hassan
sondrahassan.com

Hank D. Herring, wood stamp craftsman
hankdherringart.com

Kyra E. Hicks
BlackThreads.blogspot.com

Phyllis Hildreth, Falcon Feather Fibers
falconfeatherfibers.net

Joan Hodges
longislandtraditions.org/artistprofiles/ethnic/hodges.html

Dorothy Holden
allianceforamericanquilts.org/qsos or go directly with: bit.ly/dmhr6L

Lawana Holland-Moore
hahawater.blogspot.com

Henry Holmes
henrysarts.weebly.com

Nalo Hopkins, Canadian-Caribbean fabric designer
spoonflower.com/profiles/nalo_hopkinson

Connie R. Horne
conniehorne.com

Raymond K. Houston
nachograndmasquilts.com   nachograndmasquilts.blogspot.com

Sandi Howell
indigo6g-renaissancewoman.blogspot.com

K. Grace Howes
redbarn-studios.com/blog

Sonji Hunt
sonjihunt.com sonjisays.blogspot.com

Clementine Hunter (1886 – 1988)
folkartlife.com/articles/clementinehunter.shtml

Esther Iverem
legacyquiltsandart.com

Lynette Jackson, African American Quilting Part 1 of 4 video
youtube.com/watch?v=WS9dnotnqys

Marla A. Jackson
marlaquilts.com
allianceforamericanquilts.org/qsos or go directly with: bit.ly/9qFzw8

Céleste B. Janey
yellowrose.biz

Kiandra Johnson Jimenez
quejimenez.typepad.com/quejimenez

JlewisBlessing
sewnonmymind.blogspot.com

Jeffie Johnson, quilt pattern designer
sewfabulous.com

LaVerne Kemp
thewarpedweaver.blogspot.com

Toni Kersey
tonikersey.com

Sharon A. Keyser-Jackson, textile artist
skcreationsllc.blogspot.com

Eva D. King
allianceforamericanquilts.org/qsos or go directly with: bit.ly/9knoCe

Arianne King-Comer, indigo artist
ariannekingcomer.com

Bev Kirk
bquiltin.blogspot.com

Ora Kirkland (1918 – 2003)
www.nyfolklore.org/pubs/voic29-1-2/obit.html

Kweli Kitwana, fabric designer
africanamericanfabrics.blogspot.com
spoonflower.com/profiles/kkitwana

Catherine Lamkin
allianceforamericanquilts.org/qsos or go directly with: bit.ly/cE0EJ0

Juanita Lanaux
fiberpassion.blogspot.com

Kit Lang, Ontario, Canada
divaquilts.com

Lena's Daughter
lenasdaughter.blogspot.com

Ebony Love, Crafts Techniques Columnist, *Handmade News*
handmadenews.org/columnist/index.php?aid=77   lovebugstudios.com

Lovey, fabric collage artist
fabricphotomemories.blogspot.com

Ronke Luke-Boone, author, *African Fabrics: Sewing Contemporary Fashion With Ethnic Flair*
rlboone.com

Aisha Lumumba, Journey of an African American Quilt Artist video
youtube.com/watch?v=0tobn9KHyHo
obaquilts.com   obaquilts.blogspot.com

Evelyn Brown Macklin
thetravelingquiltboutique.com

Gwendolyn Magee
gwenmagee.com   creativityjourney.blogspot.com

Keith Mallett, fabric panel designer
keithmallett.com

Wendy Mamattah
braidandstitch.com

Ila Martin
quiltsbyila.com

Gwen Maxwell-Williams
gwenmaxwell-williams-studiog.com

Carolyn Mazloomi, author, *Spirits of the Cloth: Contemporary African American Quilts*
carolynlmazloomi.com
allianceforamericanquilts.org/qsos or go directly with: bit.ly/dax0qG

Dindga McCannon
art-alive.com/dindga

Barbara Ann McCraw
www.quiltasart.com

Mary McFairland, Quilting From the Heart video
youtube.com/watch?v=teNJWVdV5G8

Althea McNish, British textile designer
mcnishandweiss.co.uk

S. Epatha Merkerson
popmatters.com/pm/tools/print/55825

Ed Johnetta Miller
edjohnetta.com

Ruth E. Miller
ruthequiltsandthings.net

Nadine Mills, the Fabric Peddler store
thefabricpeddler.com

Tonia Mitchell
toniamitchellgallery.com

Roy Mitchell, Jr.
allianceforamericanquilts.org/qsos or go directly with: bit.ly/a061e5

Patricia A. Montgomery
dragonartplace.com

Jacquelyn Hughes Mooney
iiammoon.blogspot.com

Revil Mosely, The Quilters of Gee's Bend, Alabama Clip 1
youtube.com/watch?v=eLxIGZNLt_Q

Cynthia Yemanya Napue
yemanyanapue.com

Marlene O'Bryant-Seabrook
marleneobryantseabrook.com
allianceforamericanquilts.org/qsos or go directly with: bit.ly/clc9YX

Charlotte Hill O'Neal, Tanzania, East Africa
uaacc.habari.co.tz

Shirley Parker-Benjamin
eziliarts.com

Edna J. Patterson-Petty
fabricswork.com

Cecelia "Cely" Pedescleaux
celysquilts.com

Liz Pemberton
wix.com/lizpemberton/textiles

K. Joy Ballard Peters
njoysart.com

Tinnie Pettway, author, *Gee's Bend Experience*
geesbend.net

Phyllis
divaworksblog.blogspot.com

Barbara Pietila
africanamericanartquilt.com/gallery_pietila.html

Valarie Poitier
msvpoitier.blogspot.com

Sonja Polk, Prince Ileeoz
princeileeoz.blogspot.com

Theresa Polley-Shellcroft
studioone-artworks.net
allianceforamericanquilts.org/qsos or go directly with: bit.ly/bUORDR

Pat Porche
porchedesigns.blogspot.com tapintoart.blogspot.com

Lynda Poole Prioleau
matlyndesigns.com

Hystercine Rankin (1929 – 2010)
bit.ly/c7aOAF

Glenda Richardson
glendarichardson.com

Riché Richardson, Portrait of the Artist 1 of 3 videos
youtube.com/watch?v=7evb7pMFiGw
richerichardsonartquilts.blogspot.com

Teri Richardson, textile artist
teririchardson.net

Tracey Rico
jaderico.com

Faith Ringgold
faithringgold.com   faithringgold.blogspot.com

Keisha Roberts
keisharoberts.com
allianceforamericanquilts.org/qsos or go directly with: bit.ly/cEzTnA

Aminah Brenda Lynn Robinson
aminahsworld.org

Marie "Big Mama" Roseman (1898 – 2004)
art.org/exhibitions/archives/2006/big-mama.htm

Sonie Ruffin, Solo Quilt Exhibit video
youtube.com/watch?v=ErYLjyVAOp0

Yasmin Sabur
yasmintoo.blogspot.com

Carole Samples, embroidery
myheartsfancy.blogspot.com

Scattered Threads
scatteredthreads-xsfriend.blogspot.com

Elizabeth Talford Scott
marylandartsource.org/artists/detail_000000135.html

Joyce J. Scott
marylandartsource.org/artists/detail_000000136.html

Sandra Scott, Cambridge, England
sandrascotttextileartist.blogspot.com

Muhjah Shakir, Bioethics Community Quilt Project
tuskegee.edu/global/Story.asp?s=6447828   bit.ly/dyEPVA

Carole Lyles Shaw
CaroleLylesShaw.com   carolelylesshaw.typepad.com
allianceforamericanquilts.org/qsos or go directly with: bit.ly/bxiyPS

Sherry Shine
allianceforamericanquilts.org/qsos or go directly with: bit.ly/bUB4S2

April Shipp, Quilts and Human Rights video
youtube.com/watch?v=idammoba2Po

Kelli Simone
hobbywhore.blogspot.com

Karen L. Simpson
lafreya.blogspot.com

John Sims, the Math Art Project
johnsimsprojects.com   bombsite.powweb.com/?p=4234

Darla Sipp-Wells, Darla's Quilt Video
youtube.com/watch?v=rekZz_37Ivs

Frank Smith, quilted paintings
FrankSmithArt.com

Mary Louise Smith
community-2.webtv.net/MARYLOUISESMITH/MARYLOUISESMITH

Rosie Smith, Rosie's Quilt Video
youtube.com/watch?v=JgdjoSW_-LE

Sandra Smith
sandrasmithquilts.com

Estella Spates
allianceforamericanquilts.org/qsos or go directly with: bit.ly/9ZcKLm

Carole Gary Staples, Honey Girl Quilt Block Patterns
mivadesigns.com

Cheryl Sterling
sterling-fiberarts.com   needleandcloth.blogspot.com

Lisa Shepard Stewart, author, *African Accents*
culturedexpressions.com

Deborah Sylvester
sylvesterartquilt.com

Don Tate II, illustrator and fabric designer
devast.blogspot.com/search?q=fabric

Rosa Tellis
ebonquilts.com

Candace Thomas
candacethomas.blogspot.com

Tangie Thomas
allianceforamericanquilts.org/qsos or go directly with: bit.ly/9UoOF6

Lucinda Toomer (1888 – 1983), 1983 NEA National Heritage Fellow
nea.gov/honors/heritage/fellows/fellow.php?id=1983_14

Maxine Townsend-Broderick
ebonyquilters.com/MaxineTownsend-Broderick.htm

Sara Trail, teenage author, *Sew with Sara*
sewsarasew.com

Lynne K. Varner, *Seattle Times* columnist writes on quilting
seattletimes.nwsource.com/html/opinion/2004052802_lynne05.html

Teresa Vega
cowriequilts.blogspot.com

Hilda Vest, Quilts and Human Rights video
youtube.com/watch#!v=uhG3S0oeJRM

Naomi Wanjiku, textile artist
naomiwanjiku.blogspot.com

Cookie Washington
allianceforamericanquilts.org/qsos or go directly with: bit.ly/dhnISi

Zenobia Washington
zenobiasart.com

Sherry Burton Ways, textile and doll artist
sankofastudio.com

Erma Weekly, Erma's Quilt Video
youtube.com/watch?v=Fd9YvXB6ZxQ

Rev. Dr. Renita J. Weems
somethingwithin.com/blog/?cat=195

Della Wells
dosfolkies.com/index.php?page=della-wells

Gussie Wells (1901 – 1994), 1991 NEA National Heritage Fellow
nea.gov/honors/heritage/fellows/fellow.php?id=1991_14

Yvonne Wells
alabamaarts.org/wells.html

Sherry Whetstone-McCall
tlitor.com/Website/Sherry.htm

Beverly Ann White, Quilts and Human Rights video
youtube.com/watch?v=4L7Eefjr2ts

Ethel White
wiquiltmuseum.com/ethel_white.htm

Irma White
squidoo.com/irmawhite

Valerie C. White
valeriecwhite.com
allianceforamericanquilts.org/qsos or go directly with: bit.ly/b8Pwf3

Rochleigh Z. Wholfe, performance and visual artist, *My Name Is Harriet: The Three Faces of Courage, Integrity and Grace* (Harriet Tubman, Harriet Jacobs, and Harriet Powers)
wholfe.myexpose.com

Anna Williams
straw.com/equilters/annawilliams/index.html

Arbie Williams (1916 – 2003), 1991 NEA National Heritage Fellow
nea.gov/honors/heritage/fellows/fellow.php?id=1991_15

Carol Williams
quiltsandsewon.net

Sheila Williams
sheilawilliams.com

Trish Williams
handworksbytrish.com

Deborah Willis
en.wikipedia.org/wiki/Deborah_Willis

Sherise Marie Wright
thesoulofquilting.blogspot.com

Juanita Yeager
juanitayeagerartquilts.homestead.com

DeBorah Amoafo Yeboah
artthroughmyeyes.com

Yetunde
sistahstitchalot.blogspot.com

Annie Mae Young
anniemaeyoung.com

Sauda Zahra
allianceforamericanquilts.org/qsos or go directly with: bit.ly/92TWd1

Quilt Organizations and Guilds

54-40 African American Quilters Guild of VA
5440quilters.com

African American Quilt and Doll Guild, Warrensville Heights, OH
aaqdg.org

African American Quilt Guild of Oakland, CA
aaqgo.org

African-American Quilters and Collectors Guild
aaquiltersguild.org

African American Quilters Group, Let's Grow to 1,000,000
facebook.com/group.php?gid=234346214039

African American Quilters of Baltimore, MD
aaqb.org

African-American Quilters of Los Angeles, CA
easysite.com/aaqla

African American Quilters Gathering, Harrisburgh, PA
africanamericanquiltersgathering.blogspot.com

Benjamin Banneker Historical Park and Museum, Baltimore, MD
See the unveiling of the *Banneker Historical Quilt.*
youtube.com/watch?v=B5dkpD-7b8w

Blue Triangle Quilt Guild, Houston, TX
bluetrianglequiltguild.com

Brown Sugar Stitchers Quilt Guild, Decatur, GA
quiltsites.com/brownsugarstitchers.htm

Clara Ford Foundation
clarafordfoundation.org

Ebony Quilters of Southeast Queens, NY
ebonyquilters.com

Ebony Stitchers, Decatur, GA
ebonystitchersquiltguild.org

Gee's Bend Quilters
quiltsofgeesbend.com

Great Lakes African American Quilters Network
greatlakesaaquilters.tripod.com

Haiti Peace Quilts
haitipeacequilts.org

Harlem Needle Arts, Inc.
facebook.com/pages/Harlem-Needle-Arts-Inc/211930855511

The "Liberia's Hope" Quilting Initiative, The Corporation for Economic Opportunity
prosperityforall.org/WestAfricaInitiatives.html

Mississippi Cultural Crossroads
win.net/kudzu/crossroa.html

Needles & Threads Quilters Guild, Chicago, IL
chicagontqg.com

Needle Rules! Society of Detroit, MI
needlerules.tripod.com

Pacific Northwest African American Quilters
pnwaaq.com

Quilters of Color Network of New York
qcnny.org

Quilters of the Round Table, Philadelphia, PA
qrtphilly.com

Rocky Mountain Wa Shonaji Quilt Guild, Denver, CO
washonaji.org

San Diego People of Color Quilt Guild
easysite.com/sdpoc

Sisters in Stitches Joined by the Cloth, Holbrook, MA
sistersinstitches.org

Sisters of the Cloth Quilting Guild, Fort Wayne, IN
sites.google.com/site/testsocqg

Stitches From the Soul-Sistahs, Toledo, OH
stitchesfromthesoulsistahs.webs.com

Tutwiler Quilters, Tutwiler, MS
tutwilerquilters.org

Uhuru Quilters Guild, Clinton, MD
uhuruquiltersguild.org

Women of Color Quilters Network
wcqn.org

Zamani Soweto Sisters, South Africa
brixton50.co.uk/zamani-soweto-sisters-textile

Zuri Quilters Guild, Nashville, TN
zuriquiltersguild.blogspot.com

A special thanks to Astrid Hacker and Gwen Magee for their assistance in compiling these lists.

My goal is to be as inclusive as possible, but this list undoubtedly has unintentional omissions. If you would like to share the online addresses of other African American quilter websites, blogs or videos for future updates of this book, feel free to email me at Black.Threads@yahoo.com.

Art Quilt Blocks

What better way to celebrate the news that there are 1.6 million African American quilters in the United States than by quilting? Francine Haskins, a full-time artist, doll maker, and quilter, designed the following six art quilt blocks in celebration of the occasion.

Haskins is a native of Washington, D.C. and a graduate of the Corcoran School of Art. For years she taught hand-stitched cloth doll making classes in her studio at 1800 Belmont Street NW, a converted Victorian home in Washington, D.C., which housed several African American artists' studios, galleries and arts-related retail shops. A year after the home closed in 2000, Haskins moved her studio and classes to Belmont Arts East/The Graham Collection, a shared gallery and retail space, until it closed in 2007. Haskins continues to teach classes and to exhibit in the D.C. area.

Haskins is also the author and illustrator of two children's books. The first is *I Remember "121,"* describing her experiences from age three to nine in a close-knit Washington, D.C. neighborhood. The second book is *Things I Like About Grandma*, about a young girl's close relationship with her grandmother.

Haskins learned to machine sew in a junior high school home economics class where one of her first creations was an apron. Her mother, Frances Haskins, taught her how to sew by hand.

Haskins' art style is fresh, lively, and afro-centric.

"People look at stuff and see flat colors – red, yellow, blue," says Haskins. "They don't see different lines and textures. I see the details and layers. I see beyond what others see. I sew and quilt as another way of painting without getting things framed. I love textiles and fabrics."

The six quilt blocks Haskins designed are for intermediate and expert quilters, though one can simplify the patterns by using only the main silhouette, not the detailed interior designs. The blocks can also be used as redwork embroidery patterns.

I hope you enjoy the quilt block patterns on the next few pages. If you make a fabric block or quilt using the designs, do feel free to send a photo of your work to be showcased on the Black Threads blog!

Block #1 – Pleasant Angel

Block #3 – African Drummer

Block #5 – Eccentric Doll

Block #6 – Apple Picker

Bibliography

The following published resources focus primarily on African American quilters: autobiographies, biographies, exhibit catalogs and in-depth research. These works help us to understand what may motivate 1.6 million Black quilters to stitch, provide insights to the creative process, and showcase selected quilts.

Books, Articles and Selected Exhibition Catalogs

Beardsley, John. Gee's Bend: The Women and Their Quilts. Atlanta, GA: Tinwood Books, 2002. 336 p.

Benberry, Cuesta. Always There: The African-American Presence in American Quilts. Forewords by Jonathan Holstein and Shelly Zegart. Louisville, KY: The Kentucky Quilt Project, Inc., 1992. 132 p.

Brewer, Tina Williams, Samuel W. Black, and Laura Horner. Guided by the Ancestors. Pittsburgh, PA: Pittsburgh Filmmakers, 2009. 62 p. Catalog includes biographic sketch of Brewer and images of more than forty quilts. You can order your copy for $30 total ($25 book + $5 s/h) by contacting Jen Carter, Shop Manager, 412-361-0873 or by sending an email to shop@pittsburgharts.org.

Brownlee, Andrea B., Gloria J. W. Gayles, Leslie King-Hammond, and Amalia K. Amaki. Amalia Amaki: Boxes, Buttons, and the Blues. Washington, D.C.: National Museum of Women in the Arts, 2005. 135 p.

Callahan, Nancy. The Freedom Quilting Bee. Tuscaloosa, AL: University of Alabama Press, 1987. 256 p. History of the rural quilting cooperative from 1966 through the mid-1980s. Follows the group's development and commercial efforts to obtain a Sears contract and, later, to make the "Largest Quilt in the World." Book includes profiles of original Bee members Minder Pettway Coleman and Estelle Abrams Witherspoon.

Crosby, David. Quilts and Quilting in Claiborne County: Tradition and Change in a Rural Southern County. Port Gibson, MS: Mississippi Cultural Crossroads, 1999. 32 p. Available from the Mississippi Cultural Crossroads, 507 Market Street, Port Gibson, MS 39150.

Cubbs, Joanne, Matt Arnett, Dana Friis-Hansen, Paul Arnett, and E. W. Metcalf. <u>Mary Lee Bendolph, Gee's Bend Quilts, and Beyond</u>. Atlanta, GA: Tinwood Books, 2006. 71 p.

Cunningham, Joe. <u>Men and the Art of Quiltmaking</u>. Paducah, KY: American Quilter's Society, 2010. 112 p. Thirty male quilters and their work are profiled. The only African American male quilter included is Raymond K. Houston of St. Louis, Missouri.

Dawson, C. Daniel. <u>Family Medicine: The Art of Elizabeth Talford Scott</u>. Washington, D.C.: Anacostia Museum, 1997. 20 p. Includes extensive description of Scott's life story and artistic visions. Six full-color photographs of Scott's quilts are also included.

Ezell, Nora McKeown. <u>My Quilts and Me: The Diary of an American Quilter</u>. Introduction by Gail Trechsel. Preface by Hank Willett. Montgomery, AL: Black Belt Press, 1999. 192 p. Nora Ezell, a 1992 Fellow in the National Endowment for the Arts program, received the Alabama Folk Heritage Award in 1990. Fascinating insights into her creative process.

Flomenhaft, Eleanor, curator. <u>Faith Ringgold: A 25 Year Survey</u>. Hempstead, NY: Fine Arts Museum of Long Island, 1990.

Freeman, Marjorie Diggs, Rosalind M. Wallace, and Veronica Cartwright, eds. <u>African American Quilt Circle of Durham, North Carolina</u>. Durham, NC: AAQC Publishing, 2007. 84 p. The book includes the history of the guild and profiles of the following thirty-four members: Edna Alston, Annette Bailey, Marjorie Barner, Jerome Bias, Willa Brigham, Shirley Bullock, Veronica Carlisle, Kimberly Cartwright, Nancy Cash, Ida Couch, Tenna Crawshaw, Melanie Dantzler, Lenoia Dorris, Delores Benton Evans, Marjorie Diggs Freeman, Jan Garrett, Ife B. Grady, Hanunah Habeebullah, Doretha Hamidullah, Veronica Hicks, Roxanne Higdon, Joan McCoy, Otelia Newsome, Pauline Parker, Robin Pinchback, Jacqueline Richardson, Shirley Royal, Hattie Williamson Schmidt, Linda Steel, Linda Tate Suiter, Selena Sullivan, Candace Thomas, Patricia Walters, and Sauda Zahra. The book is $29.95 + U.S. shipping & handling ($6.75). Contact the African American Quilt Circle, 4706 High Meadow Road, Durham, NC 27712.

Freeman, Roland L. <u>A Communion of the Spirits: African American Quilters, Preservers, and Their Stories</u>. Foreword by Cuesta

Benberry. Preface by David B. Levine. Nashville, TN: Rutledge Hill Press, 1997. 396 p. This book was the first national survey of African American quilters. Freeman covered thirty-eight states and Washington, D.C.

_____. Something to Keep You Warm: The Roland Freeman Collection of Black American Quilts from the Mississippi Heartland. Jackson, MS: Mississippi State Historical Museum, 1981. 46 p. This catalog is one of the first solely devoted to documenting African American quilters.

Fry, Gladys-Marie. Man Made: African-American Men and Quilting Traditions. Washington, D.C.: Anacostia Museum and Center for African American History and Culture, 1998. 34 p. Featured quilters include ElRoy Atkins, Paul Buford, Charles Cater, Thomas Covington, Raymond Dobard, David Driskell, Benjamin Jackson, Dennis Jones, Thomas Mack, Jeff Martin, Herbert Munn, Charles Palmer, Joe Washington, and Warren Wise.

Galvin, Sean. What's This Got to Do With Quilting?: Nine Stories of Southern Women Quilters Living in New York City. Albany, NY: Lane Press, 1995. 24 p. The Elder Craftsmen Textile Project 1989 – 1994. Includes a story about the Southern African-American Quilters, a sewing group in Brooklyn. Artists include Fannie Roberts Chaney, Georgia Clark, Trannie Mae Cooper, Vivian Evans, Virginia Hall, Eunice Morgan, Mollie Rieves, Mary Ruffin and Marian Webber.

German, Sandra K. "Surfacing: The Inevitable Rise of the Women of Color Quilters' Network." In Uncoverings 1993: The Research Papers of the American Quilt Study Group, ed. Laurel Horton, pp. 137 – 168. San Francisco: American Quilt Study Group, 1994. The essay "identifies the attitudes and perceptions of some American quiltmakers who feel that barriers exist between themselves and the mainstream." It also recounts the evolution of the Women of Color Quilters' Network, a national organization dedicated to preserving African American quiltmaking. Founding members included Claire E. Carter, aRma Carter, Cuesta Benberry, Melodye Boyd, Michael Cummings, Peggie Hartwell, and Marie Wilson. German reviews the results of a 1992–93 survey in which Black quilters indicated they had low expectations for fairness, acceptance, and success from traditional or mainstream quilting ventures (e.g., quilt guilds, magazines, contests).

Grier, Rosey. Needlepoint for Men. New York: Walker & Co., 1973. 158 p. Former New York Giants and Los Angeles Rams football player shares his passion for needlepoint in this instructional book. Photos of projects completed by Grier, other men and boys are included.

Hamm, Louise. One Stitch At a Time: Photography of The Needle Rules! Society. Blurb.com, 2009. 24 p. Documentation of an inter-generational quilting session.

Hicks, Kyra E. Black Threads: An African American Quilting Sourcebook. Jefferson, NC: McFarland & Co, 2003. 260 p.

Johnson, Christina and Walter H. Johnson. Christina E. Johnson Fiber Artist and Quilter. Blurb.com, 2008. 40 p. Documents Johnson's artwork on exhibit at Villanova University, August 23 – October 4, 2007. Many pieces were inspired by her 2002 trip to Ghana.

Keckley, Elizabeth. Behind the Scenes, by Elizabeth Keckley, Formerly a Slave, but More Recently Modiste and Friend to Mrs. Abraham Lincoln, or Thirty Years a Slave and Four Years in the White House. New York: G. W. Carleton, 1868. One can also print a copy from Gutenberg.org/etext/24968.

King-Hammond, Leslie. Gumbo Ya Ya: Anthology of Contemporary African-American Women Artists. New York: Midmarch Arts Press, 1995. 352 p. Includes profiles of textile artists and quilters Xenobia Bailey, Carol Ann Carter, Julee Dickerson-Thompson, Viola Burley Leak, Faith Ringgold, and Joyce Scott.

Klassen, Teri. "Representations of African American Quiltmaking: From Omission to High Art," Journal of American Folklore, Vol.122, No. 485, Summer 2009, pp. 297-334.

Leon, Eli. Arbie Williams Transforms the Britches Quilt. [California]: Regents of the University of California and the Mary Porter Sesnon Gallery, University of California, Santa Cruz, 1993. 12 p.

_____. Something Pertaining to God: The Patchwork Art of Rosie Lee Tompkins. Shelburne, VT: Shelburne Museum, 2007. 30 p. Profile and quilts by Tompkins (1936 – 2006), whose real name was Effie Mae Howard. Contact shelburnemuseumstore.org to order. Retail price: $12.95.

_____. Who'd A Thought It: Improvisation in African-American Quiltmaking. Preface by Robert Ferris Thompson. San Francisco, CA: San Francisco Craft and Folk Art Museum, 1987. 88 p. Quilters featured include Sherry Byrd, Charles Carter, Willia Ette Graham, Angelia Tobias, Rosie Lee Tompkins, and others.

MacDowell, Marsha. African American Quiltmaking in Michigan. East Lansing, MI: Michigan State University Press, 1997. 162 p. More than 140 photographs of quilts, quiltmakers, and quilt-making activities. Essays cover the history and meaning of quilting in Michigan quilters' lives, community, and family. Cuesta Benberry provides a brief history of African American quilting. Darlene Clark Hine provides a context for examining quilting as part of Black women's cultural history. Included are interviews with quilters Deonna Green, Carole Harris, Rosa Parks, and Ione Todd.

Magee, Gwendolyn A., René Paul Barilleaux, Cuesta Benberry, and Roland L. Freeman. Journey of the Spirit: The Art of Gwendolyn A. Magee. Jackson, MS: Mississippi Museum of Art, 2004. 61 p.

Mazloomi, Carolyn. Stitching a Culture Together: African American Quilters of Ohio. Athens, OH: Ohio University Press, forthcoming 2011. 128 p.

Miller, Ed Johnetta and Curlee R. Holton. Weaving a New World: The Art of Ed Johnetta Miller. Easton, PA: David A. Portlock Black Cultural Center, Lafayette College, 2001. 6 p. Exhibit held February 2 – March 2, 2001.

Miller, Rosemary E. Reed Threads of Time: The Fabric of History: Profiles of African American Dressmakers and Designers, 1850-2002. Washington, D.C.: Toast and Strawberries Press, 2006. 280 p. This book includes thirty-eight profiles of Black designers and textile artists, including quilters Viola Burley-Leak, Elizabeth Keckley, and Rosa Parks.

Ringgold, Faith, Judith K. Brodsky, Ferris Olin, Tanya Sheehan, and Michele Wallace. Declaration of Independence, Fifty Years of Art by Faith Ringgold. New Brunswick, NJ: Institute for Women and Art, Rutgers University, 2009. 56 p. 72 ill.

Ringgold, Faith. We Flew Over the Bridge: The Memoirs of Faith Ringgold. New York: Bulfinch Press, 1995. 288 p. A remarkable autobiography of a grand artist and a must-have for those interested in how art and economics can be stitched together.

Simmons, Hilda. Crossing Borders: A Collection of Quilts to Challenge the Conventions of the Venerable Art Form. Blurb.com, 2010. 152 p.

Heartwarming book written by Simmons and her children. Simmons was born in Cuba in 1929. As the book says, she "likes to refer to herself by her full name: Hilda Rosa Céspedes Gonzales Rivalta Perez Sanchez Bernal de Simmons." She learned to sew at school and from her mother, who was a seamstress. As a child, Simmons also worked at a local photography studio taking pictures, mixing chemicals, and hand-coloring prints. In 1951, she moved to the United States and married Jonathan Simmons six years later. The couple had five children, including the oldest, Diana, a quilter. When Diana passed away at the age of twenty-five, Simmons vowed to complete Diana's unfinished quilt. This quilt would be the first Simmons ever made. This book includes photographs of many of the seventy-five quilts Simmons would come to stitch.

Smith, Julia R., and Benjamin Speller. African American Family Quilts of Bertie County, NC. Windsor, NC: Historic Hope Foundation, 2003. 14 p. Historic Hope Plantation exhibit held Feb. 15 – 28, 2003.

Turner, Patricia A. Crafted Lives: Stories and Studies of African American Quilters. Foreword by Kyra E. Hicks. Jackson, MS: University Press of Mississippi, 2009. 216 p. Quilters profiled include Elliott Chambers, Marion Coleman, Cyré Cross, Ora Knowell, Ed Johnetta Miller, Daisy Anderson Moore, Riché Richardson, Jeanette Rivers, and Tiffanie Newton Williams. Additionally, essays examining the controversy surrounding the quilts of Gee's Bend and so-called quilts from the Underground Railroad are also included.

Varner-Hollie, Lynne K., and Deborah Boone. Edited by Gwen Maxwell-Williams. Stories That Cover Us: Meditations and Fiber Art by the Pacific Northwest African American Quilters. Blurb.com, 2009. 78 p. Catalog for exhibit held March 1- October 4, 2009 at the Northwest African American Museum. Included are quilts and biographical sketches of the following quilters: Patricia Batiste-Brown, Deborah Boone, Carol Flanagan-Frank, Iris Franklin, Lynnette Gallon-Harrell, Antoinette Hall, Annie Harper, Antoinette Lewis Bush, Oneda Elizabeth Harris, Cheryl Haskins, Chistine Jordan-Bell, Donna Kimbrough, Paula Maranan, Gwen Maxwell-Williams, Johnnie Miller, Wadiyah Nelson-Shimabukuro, Vera Patterson, Lynne K. Varner-Hollie, Brenetta Ward, and Marilyn Wilson-Hanseling.

Vaz, Kim M. The Woman with the Artistic Brush: A Life History of Yoruba Batik Artist Nike Davies. Armonk, NY: M.E. Sharpe, 1995.

137 p. Fascinating life story of a young Nigerian woman who ran away from home, married into a polygynous household, endured sixteen years of domestic violence, and founded an arts and culture center. Davies is today an internationally known textile artist.

Watts, Katherine and Elizabeth Walker. Anna Williams: Her Quilts and Their Influence. Paducah, KY: American Quilter's Society, 1995. 40 p.

Williams, Heather Andrea, Lyneise E. Williams, and Raquel V. Cogell. In Between Spaces: Textured Imaginings of African-American Lives: Quilts Designed and Created by Heather Williams. Chapel Hill, NC: Sonja Haynes Stone Center for Black Culture and History, University of North Carolina at Chapel Hill, 2006. 7 p.

Willis-Chew, LaVerne. Me and My Quilts. Photographs by Christina Drane. Blurb.com, 2010. 34 p. Willis-Chew, a self-taught quilter, was born in Detroit, Michigan. Upon retirement in 2002, she joined the New Prospect Missionary Baptist Church's quilting ministry. She is also a member of the Great Lakes African American Quilting Network.

Young, LaDonne. For the L.O.V.E. of FABRIC: Photography of the Needle Rules! Society by Christina Drane. Blurb.com, 2009. 26 p.

Dissertations, Theses, and Papers

The African-American Design Archive. Cooper-Hewitt, National Design Museum, The Doris and Henry Dreyfuss Study Center Library and Archive, New York, NY. The archive documents the works of contemporary African American designers and research in African American contributions to applied arts. The archive was created in 1991 and includes textile designers.

Cuesta Benberry Collection of African and African American Quilts and Quilt History. Michigan State University Museum, 2008. Additionally, the Benberry Collection of non-African American quilt ephemera at the American Folk Art Museum in New York was transferred to the MSU Museum in 2009.

Blondin, Jill E. The African-American Quilt Experience As Cultural Regionalism. M.A. thesis. University of Illinois at Urbana-Champaign, 1996. 68 p.

Campbell, April. Mrs. Arester Earl, Black Quilter. Senior Essay. Yale College, 1978.

Campbell, Denise M. Quilting a Culture: Theories of Aesthetics, Representation, and Resistance in African American Quiltmaking. Ph.D Diss. Claremont Graduate University, 2006. 289 p.

Carpenter, Frances B. Therapeutic Dimensions of African-American Quiltmaking. M.A. thesis. Smith College School for Social Work, 1990. 77 p.

Celebrating the Life of Carrie L. Morris: A One Woman Quilt Show at the Storytellers in Cloth Seventh Annual Retreat. Eight-page stapled handout, which includes an essay by Morris on her quilting experiences and an exhibit list of more than twenty of her quilts. The show took place November 7 – 10, 2002 in Southbury, CT at the Heritage Inn. Morris' family includes four generations of quilters, including her mother, Carrie E. Grimes, her daughter, Sandy Bright, and her granddaughter, Stephanie Bright.

Davidson, Qadira. An Examination of Three African American Quilters in Florida. Ph.D Diss. Florida State University, 2010. 268 p. The art quilters profile are Lauren Austin, Lynette Johnson, and Doris George Manning.

Douah, Remi Kouessi-Tanoh. In Her Own Words: Uncovering a Life Experience Woven into the African American Quiltmaking

Tradition. Ph.D Diss. University of Minnesota, 2006. 150 p. Profiles Minnesota quiltmaker Wilma Gary, who practiced the craft for forty-seven years.

Franklin, Delner. Aunt Onie's Quilt. Paper. Yale College, 1978.

Hazard, Peggy Jean. Comforts of Home: African-American Quilts in Tucson, Arizona. M.A. thesis. University of Arizona, 1993. 174 p. Investigates influences on Black quilt-making aesthetics including African influences, quilt history, economics, mass media. Examines quilts by six contemporary Black women in Tucson, Arizona: Michele Butler, Ella Guillory, Fanny Harris, Wilma Lee, Betty Williams and "Shirley Jackson," a pseudonym for a woman who preferred not to be identified by her real name.

Hess, Janet Berry. Paternational, Community and Resistance: The African American Quilt. M.A. thesis. University of Iowa, 1992. Explores quilting traditions of American slaves.

Holmes, Peter. Alice Bolling and the Quilt Fence: Afro-American Quilting in Rural Virginia. Student Paper. Yale College, 1977.

Hood, Yolanda. African American Quilt Culture: An Afrocentric Feminist Analysis of African American Art Quilts in the Midwest. Ph.D Diss. University of Missouri-Columbia, 2000. 182 p. Includes profiles and quilts by Midwest quilters NedRa Bonds, Kyra E. Hicks, Edna Patterson-Petty, and Sherry Whetstone-McCall.

Irving, Sharon. African-Canadian Quilts of Southern Ontario 1840–1920. M.A. thesis. Cooper-Hewitt, National Design Museum and Parsons School of Design, 2000.

Johnson, Pearlie Mae. African American Quilts: An Examination of Feminism, Identity, and Empowerment in the Fabric Arts of Kansas City Quilters. Ph.D Diss. University of Missouri, Kansas City, 2008. 265 p. Quilters include NedRa Bonds, Georgia Patton, Sonie Ruffin, and Sherry Whetstone-McCall.

Eve Riley Collection. The African American Museum, Philadelphia, PA. The collection includes quilts, china, and dolls.

Anna Russell Jones Collection. The African American Museum, Philadelphia, PA. Jones (1902–1995) owned her own studio and was a freelance wallpaper and carpet designer. She was also a member of the Women's Army Corps (WAC) in World War II. The collection includes drawings and paintings of her designs, photo albums, books and newspaper clippings. 40 linear feet.

Kunene-Pointer, Liziwe Boitumelo. Continuities of African-American Quilting Traditions in Wisconsin. M.A. thesis. University of Wisconsin, Madison, 1985. 268 p.

Mann, Natalie Mislang. Decoding Cloth: An Extension of Identity in Black American Art. M.A. thesis. San Francisco State University, 2006. 122 p. Includes references to African American quilt history, Faith Ringgold and Roland Freeman.

McDonald, Mary Anne. Because I Needed Some Cover: Afro-American Quiltmakers of Chatham County, North Carolina. M.A. thesis. University of North Carolina at Chapel Hill, 1985.

Osbourne, Lucy Thelma. Piecing a Thesis in Quilt University. M. Ed. thesis. University of Toledo, 1999. 71 p.

Parisi, Dominic. Conversations with Black Women Who Live and Quilt in Eastern Kentucky. M.A. thesis. Afro-American Studies, Yale University, 1979.

Lillian Rogers Parks Papers, Historical Society of Washington, D.C., Kiplinger Research Library. 1.45 cubic feet. Parks (1897 – 1997) was a maid and seamstress at the White House during the Hoover, Roosevelt, Truman, and Eisenhower administrations. She wrote the best-seller *My Thirty Years Backstairs at the White House*, which was later made into a TV mini-series.

Cecelia Pedescleaux Papers, 1998 – 2002, Amistad Research Center, Tulane University, New Orleans, LA. 1.0 linear foot. Collection includes a quilt and articles about Pedescleaux, a New Orleans quilter, and her techniques for integrating historical themes into quilts.

Richardson, Jeri Pamela. The Freedom Quilting Bee Cooperative of Alabama: An Art Education Institution. Ed.D Diss. Indiana University, 1969. Survey of the Freedom Quilting Bee Cooperative.

Faith Ringgold Collection, Mary McLeod Bethune Council House, National Archives for Black Women's History. 3 boxes. Articles, books, and catalogs relating to Ringgold's life and career, including her involvement with Women, Students and Artists for Black Art Liberation. Gift of Faith Ringgold, 1994.

Faith Ringgold Collection, 1964 – 1998, Special Collections, Rutgers University Libraries, New Brunswick, NJ. 18 cubic feet. Items include books, articles, catalogs, and some correspondence related to Ringgold's work as well as papers related to the People's Flag Show court case. In 1970, three artists were arrested for flag desecration. They were participating in a protest rally in support of art gallery owner Stephen Radich (1922–2007).

Roberts-Burton, Angela Lynette. Out of the Land: The Quilts of the Bendolph Family. M.A. thesis. Howard University, 2009. 51 p. Examines quilts in Mary Lee Bendolph's family.

Satchwell, Margaret Beth. Beyond Aesthetics: The Quilts of Gee's Bend and Public Experience of American Folk Culture. B.A. project. James Madison University, 2005.

Scarlett, Rheima C. Afro-American Quilt-Makers in Atlanta: A Profile and Related High School Folk Art Curriculum. M.A. thesis. Georgia State University, 1987.

Stancil, Cassandra A. Nancy Riddick's Quilts: A Model for Contextualizing African American Material Culture. Ph.D Diss. University of Pennsylvania, 1995. 442 p. Examines African American material culture using twenty surviving quilts of Nancy Hughes Riddick (1869 – 1966), the daughter of a former slave and free woman.

Wyche, Evangeline. Black Women as Artists in the Southern United States: The Quilts of Tommie McMullen. Paper. Yale College, 1978.

Films and Videos

Chouard, Géraldine and Anne Crémieux (co-directors). <u>Riché Richardson Portrait of The Artist: From Montgomery, Alabama to Paris, France</u>. 22 minutes length. Video, 2007. The documentary profiles Richardson, an artist specializing in mixed-media appliqué art quilts, and examines the elements that influence her quiltmaking.

Cross, Lauren (director). <u>The Skin Project</u>. Mae's House Production and Cross Media Group. 130, 90, and 48 minutes. Video, 2010. The Skin Quilt Project is a documentary that explores colorism in the African American community. Quilters included are Wendell George Brown, Bettina Cornelius, Carolyn Crump, Michael Cummings, Michele David, Kyra E. Hicks, Brenda Kinner-Sandles, Catherine Lamkin, Carolyn Mazloomi, Dorothy Montgomery, Mary Ann Pettway, Nancy Pettway, Rita Mae Pettway, Terry Rayford, Riché Richardson, Vermelle "Bunny" Rodrigues, Bettie B. Seltzer, Sherry Shine, Phyllis Simpson, Auian Ward, Cookie Washington, Jerona Williams, and Madeline Wright.

Goldberg, Eve, Joe Hullinger, Asher Lenz, and Andy Ostwald. <u>Virginia R. Harris: Quilt Artist</u>. Santa Rosa, CA: Cottonwood Shadow Productions, 2004. 63 minutes. Video. Includes footage of Harris' one-woman exhibition "Where Do WE Go From Here?" at Sonoma State University. Thirteen politically themed quilts are included.

Herman, Bernard. <u>Talking Quilts: Architecture and Voice in Gee's Bend Quilts</u>. 63 minutes. Videodisc. IMA lecture series. Indianapolis, IN: Indianapolis Museum of Art, 2006. Dr. Herman, art history professor and director of the Center for Material Culture Studies at the University of Delaware, discusses the Gee's Bend Quilters and their creations in the context of history.

Irving, David K. (director), and Linda Freeman. <u>Faith Ringgold: The Last Story Quilt</u>. 28 minutes. Chappaqua, NY: L&S Video, 2006. Originally released in 1991.

Martinez, Esperanza G., and Linda Roennau (producers). <u>The Cloth Sings to Me</u>. 16 minutes. Video, 1995. Distributed by Filmmakers Library, 124 East 40th Street, New York, NY 10016. Phone: 212-808-4980. The video features "ebullient women quilters who display their colorful creations." Includes interviews with textile historian Floris Cash, art historian Willis "Bing" Davis and quilters Valerie Jean Bailey, Hazel Blackman, Adrienne Cruz, Marcia Goldman, Peggie

Hartwell, Betty Leacraft, Mary McAllister, Aline Moyler, and Marlene O'Bryant-Seabrook.

_____. The Spirit of the Individual. 22 minutes. Video, 1997. Distributed by Filmmakers Library, 124 East 40th Street, New York, NY 10016. Phone: 212-808-4980. Features quilters Michael Cummings and Peggie Hartwell.

Mazloomi, Carolyn, and Caryl Schuetz. Threads of Time: Quilting Show and Tell. 85 minutes. Video. IMA lecture series. Indianapolis, IN: Indianapolis Museum of Art, 2006. Women of Color Quilters Network founder Carolyn Mazloomi discusses "the unique culture and imagery that influence contemporary African American quilt-making." Quilt appraiser Caryl Schuetz discusses quilt value and collectibility.

Vadim, Vanessa, and Matthew Arnett. The Quilts of Gee's Bend. 28 minutes. DVD. Atlanta, GA: Tinwood Media, 2006. Documentary profiling quilters of Gee's Bend.

About the Author

Kyra E. Hicks is a quilter. Her creations have appeared in more than forty exhibits in the United States and abroad. She loves historical, investigative research and rediscovering the lives of quilters past. Since 2006, she has hosted a blog on African American quilting news BlackThreads.blogspot.com.

Kyra holds an MBA from the University of Michigan, a diploma from the London School of Economics and Political Science, and a BBA from Howard University. She works for Marriott International and lives in Arlington, Virginia, where she tends her colorful, fragrant rose garden.

Author's Note

I hope you enjoyed this booklet. Thank you for your support of my continued research in the area of African American quilting. Do feel free to drop me a note, share your favorite quilter or guild websites, or let me know whether you'd like to be on the mailing list when my next book is published.

Kyra E. Hicks
3037 S. Buchanan Street
Arlington, VA 22206-1512
Black.Threads@yahoo.com

More Books by Kyra E. Hicks

This I Accomplish: Harriet Powers' Bible Quilt and Other Pieces
ISBN: 978-0-9824796-5-0

The powerful quilts of Harriet Powers (1837-1910), a former Georgia slave, continue to capture our imagination today. Thousands of visitors to the Smithsonian National Museum of American History and the Museum of Fine Arts, Boston have stood transfixed viewing her *Bible Quilt* and *Pictorial Quilt*.

Until now, no one has told the entire, dramatic story of how these quilts (one sold for $5) were cherished in private homes before emerging as priceless national treasures.

"Wow! I kept leaping out of my chair!" said one reader.

More Books by Kyra E. Hicks

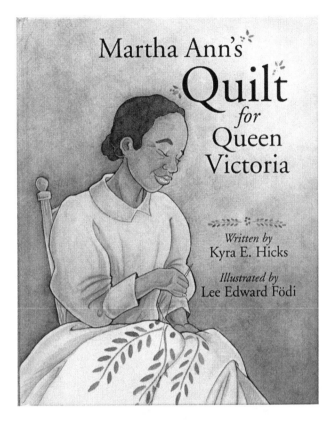

Martha Ann's Quilt for Queen Victoria
ISBN: 1-933285-59-1

Martha Ann is twelve years old when Papa finally purchases her freedom from slavery and moves the family from Tennessee to Liberia. On Market Days, Martha Ann watches the British navy patrolling the Liberian coast to stop slave catchers from kidnapping family and neighbors and forcing them back into slavery.

Martha Ann decides to thank Queen Victoria in person for sending the navy. But first, she has to save money for the 3,500-mile voyage, find a suitable gift for the queen, and withstand the ridicule of those who learn of her impossible dream to meet the Queen of England.

Visit http://bit.ly/MarthaAnnGuide for a free classroom discussion guide for grades 2–6 that you can download today.

More Books by Kyra E. Hicks

Black Threads: An African American Quilting Sourcebook
ISBN: 0-7864-1374-3

Black Threads is a comprehensive guide to African American quilt history and contemporary practices. It offers over 1,700 bibliographic references from books, articles, exhibit catalogs, and more. Also included are quilt industry estimates, a listing of African American-made quilts in 100 museums, survey results of African American quilter fabric purchasing and quiltmaking practices, and an extensive timeline covering 200 years of African American quilt history.

More Books

Liberia: A Visit Through Books
By Izetta Roberts Cooper with Kyra E. Hicks
ISBN: 978-0-557-02053-9

Izetta R. Cooper has loved books since she was a child. *Liberia – A Visit Through Books* is part biography and part bibliography. Within these covers, you will learn about the woman who lovingly raised three children and several foster children while supporting her husband's medical career, introduced the Dewey Decimal System to the University of Liberia Library, served as Library Consultant for the Presidential Library of the Executive Mansion for President William V. S. Tubman, hosted the ELTV television show, *The World of Books*, and compiled a bibliography of more than 230 historical books about her homeland.

How This Booklet Was Made

This booklet was created on a PC using Microsoft Word for the text and Excel for the tables. PDF files were produced and processed using Adobe Acrobat Pro. The interior font is New Times Roman.

Version History

1.0   August 22, 2010

LaVergne, TN USA
03 November 2010
203324LV00003B/56/P